THE WEST HIGHLAND MUSEUM

INTRODUCTION

The West Highland Museum is an independent trust with charitable status. It was founded on 23rd May 1922, without premises or a collection, only a dream: to create a museum of and for the West Highlands that was second to none in the whole country. A series of summer exhibitions, beginning with Lochaber Bygones and culminating in the brilliant 1925 Jacobite Exhibition, were organised by Victor Hodgson who personally contributed many of the exhibits and arranged for loans of interesting objects from all over the country. The exhibitions were held in the Cameron-Lucy Reading Rooms in Monzie Square and proved very popular. The Committee meanwhile were looking for permanent premises, at one time considering the Glencoe suite in the old military fort where the orders for the Massacre were signed. It was too small and not central enough, but an appeal was launched in 1925 to buy part of the present premises, from 1835 a branch of the British Linen Bank and one of the oldest buildings in Fort William. The Museum acquired it in 1926, along with a substantial mortgage that ran for 50 years.

Victor Hodgson, the guiding hand behind the museum, died suddenly in January 1929. Thanks to a Carnegie Trust Fund grant, the Committee was able to appoint its first curator, the Rev K.N. Mackenzie, but without Hodgson's enthusiasm and guidance the Museum became a little rudderless. It continued to grow however throughout the 1930s consolidating its position as *the* Jacobite Museum. During the war the exhibits were stored and some rooms used as a naval officers' mess. In the 1960s, an appeal was launched to purchase the next door building, which is now incorporated as the Education Room and an exhibition space. A huge refurbishment and upgrading was carried out in the mid 1990s, which included re-roofing the building and incorporating a new stair to improve circulation.

The *Flora MacDonald case* contains some important items such as her spinning wheel and a *Holyrood fan*. This type of fan is thought to have been given out to lady guests by Bonnie Prince Charlie, during a ball at Holyrood Palace in Edinburgh to celebrate his victory at the Battle of Prestonpans in 1745.

Ornately carved oak
settle from Callart House.

The Museum, one of the oldest in the Highlands,
is open all year round and is financed almost
entirely by admission charges. It receives a small
yearly grant from the Highland Council. Its aims
are to record, preserve and interpret items of
significance and historical interest to the West
Highland area. The collections span a wide range
of subjects from archaeology to modern industry,
with a special emphasis on the great Jacobite
risings of the 18th century.

The holdings include the Alexander Carmichael
collection, the Goldman coin collection and the
Dr Charles Hepburn bequest. The Rooms are
numbered, but there is not necessarily a specific
route to take when going round the display. This
guide gives some background
information to the main
items held by the
Museum and looks at the
general historical perspective.

The quaich is a traditional drinking vessel,
used today primarily for ceremonial purposes.

Embroidered silk waistcoat
worn by Bonnie Prince Charlie.

The table on which miscreants
were strapped to be birched -
a punishment meted out by a
policeman, accompanied by a
doctor and 'other officials'. Last
used in 1948.

THE LANDSCAPE

One of the most striking natural features of the West Highlands is the Great Glen fault, which runs south-west to north-east on a line between Fort William and Inverness. Over a period of millions of years the land-mass above the fault has 'slipped' about 65 miles. This process is on-going and small earth tremors are not uncommon.

Most of the rocks in the area are granites exposed by the erosion of the original covering layer of lava.

Ben Nevis and Glencoe were formed by 'cauldron subsidence'. A cylindrical faulting in the surface lava sank into the underlying molten rock, forcing it up into the void as granite intrusion. The summit of Ben Nevis consists of the remains of an old lava field deeply subsided into granite. This occurred after the formation of the main Caledonian mountain chain, about 400 million years ago. A considerable variety of minerals are found on the Ben. In nearby Glen Roy there are quantities of mica schist encrusted with garnet particles from which quern stones were made. These querns, used to grind oats and barley into flour, were of excellent quality and have been found far forth of the immediate locality.

Also in Glen Roy are the beaches of lakes formed when water was contained at various levels by gradually melting glaciers. There are three distinct beaches known as the Parallel Roads; flat surfaces cut into the hillsides at average heights of 1,148 ft, 1,067 ft and 848 ft above sea level. In the folklore of the area, they were the roads of the Feinne along which Fionn MacCuil, Ossian and Oscar strode.

A weather observatory was built on the 4,406 ft summit of Ben Nevis, the highest point in the British Isles. It operated for 20 years until 1904, when it was closed for lack of funds and the buildings fell to ruin. There was a pony path to the summit, up which it proved possible to take a car. Henry Alexander was the first, with a model T Ford in 1911. George Simpson, with a passenger, drove an Austin 7 up in 1928 in a record time, never beaten, of 7hrs 23mins. He made the descent in just under two hours and then drove the car home to Edinburgh! Others made the ascent by motor-bike. Earlier, in 1887, Donald MacDougal, Fort William's town crier or 'bellman' for 56 years, pushed a 73lb wheelbarrow to the top as a feat of strength.

The summit has an annual precipitation average of 161 ins, and is subject to very severe weather. In winter the staff of the observatory were quite isolated, but in summer visitors paid to walk or ride up to the hotel and post office where they recorded their comments in books now preserved in the Museum. During the two summers before the observatory was opened, Clement Wragge, accompanied by his St. Bernard dog, climbed the Ben every day to make weather recordings. His byname in the town was Inclement Wragge.

Henry Alexander driving down from the summit of Ben Nevis.

18th century watercolour of the south view of Fort William. The Fort was designed to be supplied by sea. Even after General Wade's road building programme over-land routes were difficult, if not dangerous, and water-borne transport remained vital.

Winter plumage

Summer plumage

WILDLIFE

The gannet uses its dagger-like bill to spear fish in spectacular vertical dives into the sea.

The red-throated is the most numerous of the three species of diver found in this country.

The stronghold of the golden eagle in Britain has always been the Western Highlands. The wingspan of this magnificent bird of prey can extend to over six feet.

The wildlife of Scotland includes Britain's largest native birds and mammals. A red deer stag may weigh up to 20 stone, and an adult golden eagle has a wingspan of over 6 feet. The last wolf in Lochaber is said to have been shot by a bowman in Glen Roy in about 1680. The Scottish wild cat is truly wild unlike the feral goats which are remotely descended from escaped domestic stock. A 16th century description of Loch Ness reads: *'by reason of the great woods there standing, is great store of savage beasts as harts, wild horses and roes…likewise martins, bevers, foxes and wezels, whose skins are sold unto strangers at huge prices'*. Sadly, there are no longer *bevers*, but they may yet return as they are being re-introduced into the Highlands. Seals and a large variety of sea-birds and waders can be seen on the tidal shores around Fort William.

In Lochaber, there are still remnants of native Scots pine forests, some trees being over 200 years old.

Locally, Glen Nevis is the most accessible. Natural woodlands of pine, oak and birch were cleared for settlements from earliest times and tree-felling on a massive scale began about 1600. Timber was cut for ships' masts, building and fuel, making drastic changes to the Highland landscape. Large tracts have been re-afforested mostly with non–native lodgepole pine and larch. Recently, much of the planting has been native woodland species because of encouraging Government subsidies. Having exterminated its natural predator the wolf, any new plantings have to be expensively and extensively fenced to protect them from deer.

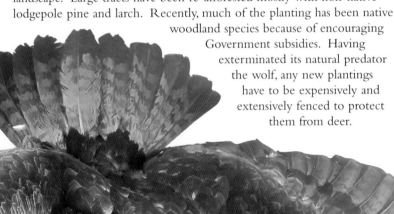

ARCHAEOLOGY

There may have been Palaeolithic peoples in Scotland, but any evidence has been destroyed by the ice of the last glaciation. Farm Fields on Rum, a Mesolithic assemblage with a later Neolithic site above it, is one of the oldest settlements known and dates to around 7,500 BC. The inhabitants exploited the bloodstone found on Rum, which could be worked like flint to form tools. Flint is only found locally in beach pebble form. Farming, using slash and burn clearance, came in around 2000 BC. Axes were then of prime importance to fell the great pine, birch and oak forests.

These Neolithic axes were of polished stone and were traded throughout Britain and Ireland. They continued in use throughout the early metalworking period, while the new technology became more efficient and durable. Made of bronze, the early type of metal axe was flat and made in stone moulds. The later hollow shapes, with a loop for more secure hafting, were cast in pottery moulds.

Bronze halberd (1300-1600 BC), found in 1960 at Leanachan.

The first metal workers, the Beaker people, buried their dead in stone cists, sometimes with grave goods and always with a small patterned pottery beaker. These burials are common in Lochaber. Later in the Bronze Age, the dead were often cremated then buried with ritual offerings of food and, occasionally, weapons or jewellery placed with them.

The Ballachulish Goddess, a 4 ft 6 ins high figure carved from alder with quartz eyes, was found on Loch Leven side in 1881. She dates to around 600 BC, the transition between the Bronze and the Iron Age. A strange, powerful presence even warped and dried out as she now is, she is a unique and enigmatic presence in the archaeological record of Scotland. She is now in the Museum of Scotland, Edinburgh.

Earthenware food vessel from a cist burial with incised design on outer bowl and rim.

6th or 7th century shoe from a crannog site.

Artist's impression of a lake dwelling.

By the first century BC, the Celts held sway in the Highlands. The vitrified forts, such as Dun Dearduil in Glen Nevis, date from this period although some may be far earlier. No authenticated example has been found south of the River Tay, and there is some doubt about their construction. Made with timber-laced ramparts dressed in stone, it is not known whether they were deliberately fired by the builders or became solidified by burning during an attack. Controlled experiments have been unable to reproduce the extensive vitrification found on these forts and they remain something of an archaeological problem.

Another type of fortification – the defensive round tower houses known as brochs – were in use before and during the first century AD, as were crannogs. Artificial islands were constructed, based on a framework of timbers then built up with wood, stones and underbrush, until a sizeable platform rose above the surface of the water to support one or more huts. The dwellings were accessible only by boat or by submerged concealed, causeways. Their use persisted into the middle ages and crannogs are recorded in Loch Lochy, Loch Ness near Fort Augustus, by Arisaig and in many other West Highland lochs. The crannog in Loch Treig was uncovered and excavated in 1933, when the dam supplying water to the British Aluminium Company was under construction.

INVERLOCHY & FORT WILLIAM

Inverlochy was the site of some epic battles most notably in 1645, when the Marquis of Montrose, in support of Charles I, defeated the Earl of Argyll's Covenanting army. Montrose said that the route, in haste and secrecy from Kilcumein (Fort Augustus) via Glen Roy, was his 'difficultest march of all' and a contemporary account records 'two dayes threw the mountains in great extremetie of cold, (&) want of wictualles…'. His force was outnumbered two to one, but at least half of Argyll's men, surprised by the attack, fell in the battle and pursuit.

The chronicler Hector Boece, whose sometimes fanciful History of Scotland was published in Latin in 1526, gives one of the earliest historical references to Inverlochy. He wrote of a town, a burgh even, flourishing some years before the Christian era, where French and Spanish merchants came for the abundant fish. No archaeological remains substantiate this. The ruins of the late 13th century curtain wall castle can be visited.

In 1654, a fort called Inverlochtie was built by General Monk for his Cromwellian troops: *'only a kind of ditch..and a few sorry wooden or clay hutts..'.* This fell into disuse after the Restoration, but in 1690 William II's Commander-in-Chief in Scotland built a new fort on the old foundations. He called it Fort William after the King. The Prince of Orange had become King William III of England at the invitation of nobles discontented with the rule of James VII and II. Scotland was less enamoured of him, but eventually he was offered the throne, becoming William II, King of Scots. Many of the West Highland clans remained loyal to James VII. To bring the Highlands to heel, William required the

This engraving of 1836 shows a fanciful version of the rout of Argyll's army, seen fleeing from Old Inverlochy Castle.

chiefs of the hostile clans to sign an oath of allegiance to him, by 31st December 1691. Most were not keen, but did so. MacIain, Chief of the MacDonalds of Glencoe, went to Fort William to sign on December 30th, 1691, but the Governor, Colonel John Hill, was not empowered to administer the oath. MacIain had to travel to Inveraray, which he reached on 2nd January, where he duly signed two days late. With full Royal approval, the Master of Stair and the Campbell Earl of Breadalbane, were determined to make an example of the clan. Instructions were issued for the Massacre of the MacDonalds of Glencoe and the reluctant Governor Hill gave the orders from Fort William to carry it out. The Argyll Regiment, many of them Campbells, a powerful, expansionist clan with a history of feuding with the MacDonalds, was billeted in the houses in Glencoe for two weeks. The Regiment was ignorant of what it was to do and the soldiers were on good terms with their hosts. The orders came through and, in the early hours of February 13th, the guests rose up and all the MacDonalds who could not escape were slaughtered. A few soldiers tried to give some warning, appalled at the abuse of the clan's trust and hospitality. MacIain himself was killed with 35 others and the survivors fled into the winter hills. Colonel Hill reported to his superiors the next day, *'I have also ruined Glencoe…their goods are a prey to the soldiers and their houses to the fire'*. By this one rank act, William II delivered the West Highland clans into the arms of the Jacobites.

A watercolour view of Fort William in 1820.

During the 1715 Rising, Fort William was garrisoned by the Sixteenth Foot (the Bedfordshire Regiment). In 1746, it was besieged by the Jacobite army under Lochiel. In preparation for this, the Fort's Governor ordered the burning of the surrounding wood and thatch houses of the little town of Maryburgh.

Fort William and Maryburgh from a hand-tinted engraving of about 1745.

After Culloden, the Fort was a centre for the troops hunting for Prince Charles Edward. By the end of the century there was no need for a closed garrison, and Parade House was built in the town for the Governor. The office lapsed in 1854, and ten years later the Fort was sold to private owners who, in 1889, sold it on to the West Highland Railway Company. A panelled room from the Governor's house in the Fort was preserved and has been reconstructed in the museum.

There was no town where Fort William stands now until the military came. The first settlement in 1654, was called Braintoun after the first Governor. In 1690, the settlement was called Maryburgh, after William II's Queen. When the Duke of Gordon became feu superior, he called it Gordonsburgh. Duncan Cameron of Callart later tried to change the name to Duncansburgh, the only survival of this being the Duncansburgh Church. In 1954, to celebrate the tercentenary, a suggestion was made to change it to Abernevis. Through all this hubris, the town remained to the locals what it had always been: *an Gearasdan,* the garrison to the Gaelic speakers and to the English speakers, the Fort.

Commemorative medals of:

'Queen'
Clementina

the Jacobite
oak emblem

the Duke of
Cumberland's victory

Cardinal York's
claim to the throne

A touchpiece
of 'Charles III'
(against the King's evil)

THE JACOBITES

The House of Stewart (or Stuart, the French spelling) ran in direct descent from Robert the Bruce through his daughter Marjory, who married Walter, High Steward of Scotland. Although some individual monarchs ruled precariously, the throne itself had strong popular support as the symbol of independent national integrity. In 1603, James VI inherited the throne of England on the death of Elizabeth I, becoming James I of England. James VII and II fled to France in 1687, having been deposed from the English throne after raising fears of an unwelcome Catholic supremacy. His Protestant daughter Mary and his son-in-law William Prince of Orange, were offered the English throne. The Scots, after intense debate and with some reluctance, agreed that James VII had forfeited his right to the throne and that they too would offer it to William and Mary. John Graham of Claverhouse, Bonnie Dundee, immediately left the Convention and raised his standard for James VII, the first act of the Jacobites in Scotland. The Jacobites were the supporters of James VII and II, so called from Jacobus, the Latin form of James. The loyal clans of the West Highlands rose with him and he decisively beat the Williamite army at Killiecrankie. Dundee was killed in the battle and the Jacobite opposition lost direction through lack of leadership. When James VII and II died at St. Germain in 1701, his 13-year old son, by his second marriage to Mary of Modena, was recognised by the Kings of France and Spain as *de jure* James VIII and III. However, his second daughter Anne, sister of William's Queen, was already the *de facto* monarch having ascended to the thrones of England and Scotland on the death of William, in 1702. She died in 1714, the last of the Stuart monarchs, having presided over the creation of the United Kingdom with the loathed union of the English and Scots Parliaments, in 1707, a political act that forced many of its opponents into the Jacobite fold. In 1715, James VIII made an unsuccessful attempt to gain the British throne. The ill-led Rising, under the Earl of Mar, ended at Sheriffmuir, a curiously indecisive battle that had no victor and no vanquished.

James VIII married Clementina Sobieska, grand-daughter of King John III of Poland, and their first son, Charles Edward Louis Philip Casimir was born in Rome, in 1720. A new star appeared on the night of his birth and was taken as a good omen for the Stuart cause. Meanwhile, the Hanoverian George I had succeeded to the United Kingdom throne. His supporters called the Stuart claimants pretenders. In 1745, Prince Charles, appointed Regent of Britain by his father, led the last Jacobite Rising. He left France with two ships, himself on board la Doutelle, with the 'Seven Men of Moidart' and 4,000 *louis d'or.* The companion vessel, the 64 gun Elizabeth, containing arms and a small French volunteer force, was so badly damaged in an encounter with the Lion, one of the British ships sent to intercept the Prince, that she had to return to Brest. The campaign was now dependent on the ability and willingness of the loyal chiefs to rally their clansmen. The prospects were not promising when Charles Edward landed

The Battle of Culloden (a few miles east of Inverness) meant the end of Jacobite hopes for the removal of the Hanoverian dynasty.

at Loch nan Uamh, on July 25th, 1745, but following the pledge of support by Lochiel, 1,200 Highlanders saw the Royal Standard raised at Glenfinnan the following month. They marched towards London, capturing Edinburgh and Carlisle and reached Derby where they turned back, largely because the English and Welsh Jacobites did not rise up in support. The only English Regiment raised was the Manchester Regiment, which drew its support from an urban base. The Jacobite Army was bitterly defeated on Drummossie Moor at Culloden, on April 16th, 1746. Post Culloden, the treatment of the Jacobites by the victorious Government troops earned their commander, William Augustus, Duke of Cumberland, a younger son of George II, the name of the Butcher by which sobriquet he is remembered to this day.

Bonnie Prince Charlie disguised at Flora MacDonald's maid, "Betty Burke".

Flora MacDonald

After Culloden, Charles Edward, with a price of £30,000 on his head, was a fugitive through the Highlands and Islands, until September when he escaped to France. Constantly in danger of arrest, at one stage he was disguised in women's clothes as Flora MacDonald's maid, Betty Burke. This was one of the many romantic episodes associated with Bonnie Prince Charlie. Personal charm and looks may have accounted for some of the fervour for the Stuart cause in 1745 but by no means all. It was 30 years since the death of Queen Anne, but however content people were under the House of Hanover, the undeniable right of the Royal House of Stuart to the throne of the United Kingdom could not be gainsaid, however undesirable its restitution might be. Despite the threat of heavy penalties, his followers pledged their loyalty to 'The King Over the Water' and even those not out with the Prince helped to hide him and engineered his escape after Culloden.

The 1745 Rising was a civil war and it is worth remembering that the worst atrocities perpetrated against the Jacobites in its aftermath were carried out by lowland Scots. By no means were all Scots Jacobite; many were strong Government supporters, both Highlanders and Lowlanders, nor were all Englishmen George's men; although their commitment when called upon proved a chimera, many of the great houses of England were Jacobite sympathisers.

There were no more risings to restore the succession, and the Bonnie Prince, exiled and without hope, became a sour, disappointed man, often drunk and violent in temper. In 1772, he married Princess Louise of Stolberg, 30 years his junior. It was a miserable marriage and without children. 20 years earlier, his mistress, Clementina Walkinshaw, had borne him a daughter, Charlotte, whom he had long neglected. In his last years in Italy he recognised and legitimised her, creating her Duchess of Albany. She became his companion and remained with him until his death, in 1788. She died herself the following year, unmarried, leaving two daughters and a son.

George IV, as Prince Regent, contributed to the cost of a marble monument commemorating Prince Charles Edward, his father James VIII and III and his brother Henry, Cardinal Duke of York. It was sculpted by Canova and stands

The likeness of Prince Charles Edward Stuart is only seen when reflected in the cylinder of this 'secret' anamorphic portrait. Ingenious devices such as this were employed to toast the Prince and the exiled Stuarts.

in St. Peter's, in Rome. Henry claimed the succession on Charles' death and died himself in 1807, *de jure* Henry I, monarch of a kingdom in which he never set foot, the last of the legitimate Stuart line.

Flora MacDonald was born in South Uist in 1722. She had returned from Edinburgh to hear the rumours of Prince Charles Edward's landing. At the end of June 1746, when he was in hiding after Culloden, she helped him to reach Skye from North Uist, where he had taken refuge in a cave. She disguised him as her maid for the hazardous journey; first a rough sea crossing in a small boat and then overland. They were always in danger from the militia patrols hunting for the Prince, who nearly gave himself away by the awkward management of his skirts. They parted at Portree and on her return to South Uist Flora was arrested. For helping the fugitive Prince for those few days, she was taken to London and kept a state prisoner, briefly in the Tower of London, but mostly just under supervision, until the Indemnity Act a year later.

In 1750 she married Alan MacDonald of Kingsburgh, whose father had been imprisoned for a year for giving aid to the Prince. He had incurred heavy financial losses because of his arrest, which severely impoverished the family. After his death, Alan and Flora emigrated to America. In 1774 they went with some of their children to North Carolina, where there was an established settlement of Highlanders, many of them MacDonalds. A ball was given in Wilmington on their arrival to welcome the Jacobite heroine. Their life was disrupted two years later by the American Revolution, when some of the newly immigrant Scots, although they had no cause to like the British Government of George III, took up arms against Washington's patriots. Flora was personally responsible for urging numbers of them to fight, and her husband, son and son-in-law fought on the Government side. Many older established Highlanders sided with their adopted country.

Alan and his son were taken prisoner and did not see Flora again until 1783. She meanwhile became the object of suspicion and reprisals. Impoverished and in poor health, she sailed from Charleston to return home in 1779. She died in Skye on 5th March 1790.

After the Jacobite defeat at Culloden, traditional Highland instruments were suppressed and legislation against them was imposed.

The Poltalloch harp, a 19th century clarsach of the Queen Mary type.

15

The Appin
Murder gun,
identified as
'the black gun
of misfortune'

THE APPIN MURDER

The Highlands were disarmed, by law if not in
practice, at the time of the notorious Appin
murder in 1752. The victim was Colin
Campbell of Glenure, King's Factor of some
Jacobite estates confiscated after the defeat at
Culloden, including that of Charles Stewart of
Ardshiel. James Stewart, guardian to Charles'
family was arrested and imprisoned in Fort
William for conspiring to the crime. He was
tried at Inveraray and hanged at Ballachulish,
protesting his innocence. A 'Long Spanish Gun'
was an important feature of the complicated and
confusing evidence. Alan Breck Stewart, officially
charged with the actual shooting, was never
brought to trial.

WEAPONRY

In the skirmishes and feuds characteristic of the
Highlands, clansmen regularly carried an array of
arms. The targe, a round shield of oak or fir
boards, occasionally even steel, covered with hide,
weighed up to 8 lbs. The centre was spiked and
the tooled designs were often picked out with
brass studs. In the relative peace before the 1745
Rising it had fallen into disuse, but when the
Jacobite army was in Edinburgh and Perth targes
were made in those cities costing from five to ten
shillings each. In the hand to hand fighting at
Culloden the Government troops used a new
and effective bayonet drill. By attacking the
man to his right rather than his direct opponent,
the soldier could get past the Highlander's targe.
Boswell wrote, *'After the disarming act they made
them serve as covers to their buttermilk barrels'*.

The Breadalbane gold dirk, seen here with the small knife and fork which fit into the scabbard.

The double edged blades of broadswords were usually imported from Germany or Italy and fitted to locally-made hilts. These became known as claymores or great swords, although the name was first given to the much older and larger two-handed swords often carved on Celtic tombstones.

The dirk is a single edged dagger and may have a small knife and fork in the scabbard. A flint-lock pistol with powder horn, a pouch to hold shot, and possibly a musket and bayonet completed the fighting man's equipment.

The Lochaber axe is a curious weapon not obviously useful to a Highlander in battle. It resembles most closely a Jeddart stave and there is a reasonable argument that they were called Lochaber axes, not because they were used here, but because the wood for the shafts came from the forests of Lochaber.

Queen Victoria presented her ghillie John Brown with a set of Highland dress accoutrements, including this dirk and sword, to mark the occasion of the wedding of her daughter Princess Louise to the Marquis of Lorne.

G. III. R.

LXXIX. REGIMENT,

OR,

CAMERON VOLUNTEERS.

All VOLUNTEERS, who wish to Serve his Majesty KING GEORGE THE THIRD,

Have now an opportunity of entering into present Pay, and free Quarters, by Enlisting into

The LXXIX. *Regiment, or, Cameron Volunteers,*

COMMANDED BY

Major *ALLAN CAMERON of ERCHT,*

Who has obtained his *Majesty's* Permission to raise a *Regiment* of *Highlanders*; which he does at his own private Expence, having no other View connected with the undertaking, except the Pride of Commanding a Faithful and Brave Band of his Warlike Countrymen, in the Service of a King, whose greatest Happiness is to reign as the Common Father and Protector of his People.

ALL ASPIRING YOUNG MEN

Who wish to be serviceable to their *King* and *Country*, by Enlisting into the *79th Regiment*, or, *Cameron Volunteers*, will be Commanded by the *Major* in Person, who has obtained from his Majesty, that they shall not be draughted into any other Regiment; and when the Reduction is to take place, they shall be marched in to their own Country in a Corps, to be therein disembodied.

The past and well known Generosity of Major *Cameron* to all his *Countrymen* who have applied to him on former occasions, is the strongest Pledge of his future Goodness to such as shall now step forward and Enlist under his Banner.

Any Young Man who wishes to Enlist into the *Cameron Volunteers*, will meet with every Encouragement by applying to the Major in Person, or, to any of the Officers, Recruiting for his *Regiment*.

GOD SAVE THE KING
AND
CONSTITUTION, AMEN.

facsimile of original Broadsheet   Hay Henderson Edin

Recruiting poster for the 79th regiment.

Early in 1778, because of the harassment of shipping on the Scottish coasts by French and American privateers (including the adventurer Paul Jones), various seaports began to form Voluntary Associations of armed men for local defence. In April the government formed the first regiments of Fencible Infantry – troops voluntarily enlisted for service in Scotland only. Those raised in 1794 were for service throughout the British Isles. These defensive regiments were usually disbanded after a few years. The Lochaber Fencibles were raised by Lochiel in 1798 and disbanded in 1802.

Cross belt plates from Fencible regiments raised during the Napoleonic Wars.

MEDALS

At the same time it was decided that more general service troops were needed. Several Scottish regiments were formed when France, after supplying arms and volunteers to America during the War of Independence, declared war on Britain.

In 1793 Alan Cameron of Erracht, a kinsman of Lochiel, was granted a charter to raise the 79th Cameronian Volunteers. He did this almost entirely at his own expense and commanded them for 15 years. He had previously fought with the Loyalists in America, having gone there after killing his opponent in a duel. The 79th paraded in Fort William before marching to Stirling, where the regiment was embodied in January 1794. The name was later changed to the Cameron Highlanders then the Queen's Own Cameron Highlanders, when Queen Victoria presented new colours in 1873. Most recently, the regiment amalgamated with the Seaforths, becoming the Queen's Own Highlanders, and these amalgamated with the Gordons to form The Highlanders.

British medals struck for general distribution as battle decorations are of comparatively recent date. Cromwell issued a medal to all the officers and men of his army after his victory at Dunbar in 1650, but the next distribution was not until Waterloo in 1815, by George IV as Prince Regent. He also instituted long service and good conduct medals for the army and navy, so the separate issue of these by individuals and regiments gradually ceased.

Medals from World War I. The bronze plaque was issued to the families of all soldiers killed in the conflict.

THE CHURCH

The early Christian Church in Scotland was a monastic tradition, stemming chiefly from Saint Columba who founded a religious community on Iona in 563 AD. By the 12th century, the Celtic Church had long been superseded by the primacy of Rome with control vested in bishops appointed by the Crown. After the Reformation in the 16th century the Episcopal Church was established, but it was rapidly overtaken by the teachings of Calvin and Presbyterianism. The Episcopal Church, like the Catholic Church, was controlled by bishops. However, the Presbyterian Church was egalitarian, drew its authority from God and saw all its ministers as equal. One problem that both reformed Churches faced was the training of sufficient priests and ministers to go out into the parishes. Both Churches had their power bases, the Episcopal Church in the north east, the Kirk in the lowlands and the south west. Other areas, including parts of the West Highlands, were untouched by the new religious thinking as no priest or minister reached them. James VI and his son Charles I tried to impose episcopacy, as Crown-appointed bishops gave control of the Church to the monarch. It was opposition to Charles I's meddling with their religious freedom that forced the Presbyterians to sign the National Covenant, in 1638. In 1643 the Presbyterian Scots entered the English civil war against Charles I while the West Highland clans, mostly Roman Catholic and Episcopalian, rose up with Montrose – ostensibly for the King, but more immediately, against the encroachments of the Presbyterian Argyll Campbells. The Royalists were defeated and both Charles I and Montrose were beheaded.

From 1638, tokens were used by both Presbyterian and Episcopalian churches, to identify those fit to receive Communion, and in times of religious persecution to keep out spies and informers. In a Glasgow parish for example, '..none had entress bot he who had ane taiken of leid, declaring that he was ane Covenanter'. Some ministers left their churches altogether and held open air meetings to which crowds of people travelled great distances. The first translation of the Bible into Highland Gaelic was made in the 17th century.

16th century brass chalice from St. Clement's Church, Rodel, Harris.

Communion Tokens from Kilmallie and Kilmonivaig parishes.

Presbyterianism became the established religion in 1592, although different interpretations gave rise to alternative versions. The Reformed Presbyterian Church, among others, sent missionaries to America, and tokens taken from Scotland in 1752 to Pennsylvania were the first ever used there. Patronage was sanctioned by Act of Parliament in 1712 and congregations had no right of choice of their minister. This provoked a series of protests, and in 1843, after declaring such Acts '*void and null*', more than 400 ministers abandoned the Establishment and formed the Free Church. In the Strontian district of Argyll, the congregation of the new breakaway church was refused land to build a place of worship. So in 1846, they had a vessel specially constructed in Greenock, which was towed to Loch Sunart and moored there. *Eaglais Iaruinn* – literally the Iron Church, but called in English the 'Floating Church', was in use for 30 years and is said to have held 700 people. Patronage ceased in 1874, but by then the disruption of the Free Church from the Establishment had become permanent.

This contemporary engraving shows the *Eaglais Iaruinn* - literally translated 'The Iron Church', being towed out into Loch Sunart in 1846. Moored in the centre of the loch, it was in use for 30 years and accommodated up to 700 people.

Inveraray penny

COINAGE

Robert III groat

The Museum has a very fine collection of pre-union coins. The oldest on display is a silver penny of William the Lion (1165-1214). There were mints at Roxburgh, Berwick, St Andrews, Edinburgh and Perth. With the accession of James VI to the English throne the coinages of the two countries became very similar, with the English types prevailing. Twelve shillings Scots equalled one shilling sterling. This difference continued until money was standardised by the articles of the Act of Union, in 1707. No Scottish coins were minted after 1709. Milled rims, to prevent the scraping of metal from the edges of gold and silver coins, were introduced in the mid-17th century and the currency of Charles II bridges the change from the hammered process, dating from Roman times, to the screwmill method of stamping the design on the metal. The Gaelic word for penny is *sgillin*.

James VII and II
ten shilling piece

Coin-like tokens were circulated by tradesmen during the 16th century because of the lack of small change, and these were at one time exchangeable for coins of the realm.

Queen Anne
sixpence

A print by Sir D.Y. Cameron from copperplate engraved for banknotes. In 1746 the sloop 'Hazard' bringing money from France was lost and the Jacobites were in such urgent need of currency that the young Robert Strange was commissioned to design and engrave plates for Prince Charles Edward's Treasurer. There were to have been notes for values up to £200 but none was issued.

SOCIAL HISTORY

Grants of land were given to various influential families by Royal Charter after the 13th century Wars of Independence, but no title was worth having without the strength to hold it and territory often changed hands by force. The history of Lochaber includes notable examples of disputes concerning ownership, and there were many clan feuds as well as reiving (cattle stealing raids) to provide for the chief's following, especially where the land was agriculturally poor. Chiefs reckoned their wealth in men, not money, and rents were generally paid in kind and in service. In return, clansmen enjoyed continuity of land tenure as 'kindly' or hereditary tenants. They had no recognised legal right of possession however, and when in the 19th century many were forcibly removed they had no redress.

After the 1745 Rising the old clan system, already under pressure in a changing world, was deliberately attacked by the Government through the forfeiture of estates and the banishment of the patriarchal chiefs who had been out. When the chiefs, or often their heirs, finally returned a generation and a half later, they came as landlords not as the fathers of their people. They came with different needs and expectations, wishing to exploit their land and make it earn them money. No longer did they need or count their wealth in men. The Government's policy was successful and the clan system was destroyed. Thus betrayed, the people began to drift away from the Highlands, some driven abroad by desire to maintain their old way of life in the form of the great tacksman emigrations of the early 19th century and latterly by starvation when the potato crops failed. Lochaber never saw the sustained landlord clearances of the North Country and Skye, but

Cameron - one of Mclan's famous plates illustrating Highland dress and clan tartans. Robert Ronald Mclan (1803 - 1856), a descendant of the MacDonalds of Glencoe, was an actor in his early years. He was a self-taught artist and his paintings, expressing his enthusiasm for the Highlands and especially his representations of Highland chiefs, have always been popular for their vigour and accuracy.

Knoydart and Morvern were severely affected. Everywhere as men left they were replaced by sheep. The Highlands have never recovered their former status as a populous though not necessarily prosperous agricultural area. Today, of 80 or so major clans many now have thriving associations and societies, mostly in the new world and the old colonies, to keep their members in touch with each other and with their history.

Although many clans traced their pedigree to an earlier date, the system was probably strongest from the 12th – 17th centuries. *Clann* means children and a chief considered himself, and was regarded as, the head of an extensive family. His blood relatives were the nucleus, but the clan stretched to include all those connected with his lands. They could choose to adopt the chief's name or keep their own sept patronymics. This produced a closely-knit interdependency of men of different means and status, fiercely loyal to their clan and chief. That is not to say that there could not be disagreement and rivalry amongst clansmen; on occasion, as in the 1745 Rising, close blood relatives were opposed and even fought on different sides, although often this was political expediency.

This detail from an 18th century Chinese porcelain plate shows two Highlanders in traditional dress. One is seen playing the bagpipes, carrying Clan colours, and the other holds a rifle.

The wearing of tartan was prohibited after the 1745 uprising, except when worn as regimental uniform. Until this time it had been the usual dress of the Highland Clans.

LIFE ON THE LAND

Croft is an Anglo-Saxon word meaning a field and survives in many place names in Scotland and England. The term 'crofter' means the holder of the smallest sub-tenancy under the old Highland system of land tenure. Groups of croft holdings are called townships. A clan chief's power once depended on the size of his following and the sub-division of land had been encouraged, often leading to poor living conditions. During the Clearances, when estate owners tried to improve the land and its revenue by removing the population and introducing large numbers of sheep, many Highlanders were forced to the lowland towns or emigrated. The crofter of today has security of tenure and usually combines a job or trade with the traditions of an older way of life.

Miss Eunice Murray assembled and dressed the collection of dolls, each representing a character with a distinctive Highland occupation. The nearest to mechanised tools are the loom and spinning wheel. The figures shown right are a crofter with cas chrom, a metal-tipped wooden foot-plough well suited to small patches of steep or stony ground, and a woman carrying a creel of peat, cut and dried for fuel. The old way was hard. Peat was in many places the only fuel. It had to be cut, stacked, turned to dry then carried back to the one-room cottages of stone or turf thatched with heather. The ground was broken for cultivation with a foot plough, and seaweed used as fertiliser was carried from the shore to the plantings. The grain harvest, cut by hand, was threshed and winnowed before being milled between two flat quern stones. The crofters kept a few sheep and small black cattle, but wool was scarce and valuable and meat not always available. Smoked or salted fish and sea-birds like gannet and comorant were staples, along with oat or barley meal, milk, butter, cheese and, from the mid 18th century, potatoes. Tea was a novelty and was at first considered dangerous.

In summer, the cattle were taken to high pasture ground by the younger members of the family who enjoyed a kind of holiday, living in shielings and making stores of butter and cheese.

These two dolls represent a traditional crofting couple: The man carries a 'cas chrom', a metal-tipped wooden foot plough, and his wife carries a creel of peat on her back.

A traditional creel.

At the end of the year, some animals were killed and their meat salted down for the winter. Before the Highlanders learned to grow a fodder crop for winter feeding, those cattle which survived the hard weather were in very poor condition, even when kept under cover in stalls at one end of the croft house. Fort William was on one of the droving routes from Skye and Lochaber to Falkirk and further south. Large numbers of sheep and cattle were driven to market in the 18th and 19th centuries. John Cameron of Corriechoille near Spean Bridge, one of the most famous drovers, was at one time reputed to own 60,000 sheep.

Wild plants provided medicines and dyes for colouring wool. Flax and even nettles were used to make linen, and women often sat spinning out of doors. Inside, smoke from the peat fire blackened the ceilings. Light was supplied by fish-oil or animal fat burning in hanging cruisie lamps. Very few people could read or write, but there was excellent entertainment to be had in tale telling, music and dancing.

Whisky bottle from the Fort William distillery founded in 1825 by 'Long John' MacDonald.

The common drink in the Highlands used to be ale brewed from native barley. In 1735, the civilian population of Maryburgh had a dispute with the Governor of Fort William about their right to brew it. The making of whisky began in the 16th century and from the early 18th century it was subject to duty. To avoid this, the spirit was often illicitly made in pot stills, carefully hidden from the excisemen. Government subsidies were offered to regularise whisky production and in 1825 'Long John' MacDonald started a distillery in Fort William. It is still in production, although the Long John name was sold to a rival firm many years ago. A great-grandson of the Keppoch chief killed at Culloden, Long John MacDonald was 6 ft 4 ins, hence the nickname. In 1835, the Minister compiling the Kilmallie parish entry in the Statistical Account recorded the absence of local demand for library books and considered that *'the numerous spirit shops in that village (Fort William)…prove a great snare to those who ought to employ their time in reading'*.

This illicit whisky still was left on the steps of the Museum in 1924 by an anonymous donor. Holes had been punctured in it by The Department of Customs and Excise.

COSTUME

The wearing of tartan was proscribed after the '45, except as regimental uniform. Until then, it was for the most part worn only by Highlanders. Later it was promoted by George IV's visit to Scotland and it became still more popular during Queen Victoria's reign. The word originally meant only a particular kind of cloth. The repeating chequered designs called setts, date from about the end of the 16th century. Many tartans are of quite recent design, while old prints and portraits often show individuals wearing a variety of setts in different articles of clothing.

The kilt in its modern form dates from the late 18th century. Previously men dressed in a shirt and plaid – a very long, untailored piece of cloth, usually tartan, of two narrow widths sewn together. The Gaelic name is derived from a Danish word meaning to gird or tuck up: *feileadh mor* for the belted plaid and *feileadh beag* for the kilt. To put the plaid on, it was laid on the ground in rough pleats on top of a belt. The wearer then lay down, in his shirt, fastened the belt around his waist, and got to his feet arranging the folds and draping the spare cloth round his shoulders, where a large round brooch held it in place. The plaid was also worn as a cloak over close fitting trews or could be used as a blanket. The sporran, made of leather, animal pelts or horsehair, is used as a purse and pocket.

Women also wore the plaid, as a shawl over plain or tartan dresses. The cloth was very dense and weather-resistant. Long strands of wool prepared for spinning with heated iron combs (as opposed to 'carded' short fibres), made a very compact yarn for hard tartan, which was deliberately shrunk or 'fulled' before use. Local plants were the source of most of the dyes, and weavers worked from traditional pattern sticks, which recorded the colours and the number of threads of the different tartan setts.

Below: Late 19th century hard tartan jacket. Kilt believed to have belonged to the Sobieski Stewarts.

A Victorian child's outfit and examples of dirks and sporrans.

Export Porcelain

At the beginning of the 18th century, china was being specially made at the factory of Ching-te-chen for the European market through agents in Canton. The much prized fine, hard paste porcelain was decorated in the traditional Chinese manner and with armorial bearings copied from customers' patterns or drawings. As the Chinese artists were quite unfamiliar with the complex heraldic devices, there were occasional errors, sometimes making it difficult to identify the owner. There were various periods of production. Practically no oriental armorial china is known after 1820; by that date the Worcester factory carried out most of the work for the French and English markets. Lowestoft is a soft paste porcelain and many pieces closely resemble Worcester. One of the plates in the Museum collection was ordered by an officer serving in Fort William, Calcutta, and another bears the arms of the last Earl of Seaforth, whose tragic life was foretold among the prophecies of the Brahan Seer.

Chinese export porcelain plate, with Mackintosh arms.

Snuff

Snuff, the roasted stalks of tobacco, ground into powder and inhaled, was very popular in Scotland among both men and women in the 18th century. Mulls and boxes were made in a variety of materials. Snuff must be kept dry, and small wooden boxes with a patent well-fitting hinge, were made in the 1800s in a number of Ayrshire villages of which Mauchline is the best known.

Horn snuff mull in the form of a raven's head.

Silver snuff box incorporating a portrait of King Charles I.

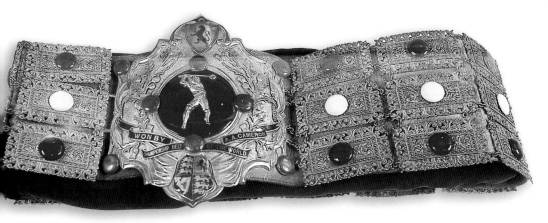

A.A. Cameron's World Championship belt.

Sport

A.A. Cameron 'Muccomer', the Lochaber athlete, won the World Championship belt for wrestling in 1903, 1904 and 1906, and held many records for feats of strength.

There is an annual race from Fort William Town Park to the summit of Ben Nevis and back, in September, which attracts runners from all over Britain. The present men's record time is just under one and a half hours.

Women have run the Ben Race almost from its inception. In 1902, Lucy Cameron from Loch Arkaigside, held the Ladies Record to the top of the Ben having run it in 2hrs 3mins.

A.A. Cameron

Champion all-round Heavyweight athlete of the World

Holder of the following Records.

PUTTING THE BALL

16	–	(7ft. 6 ins. run)	–	55ft.	6	ins
18	–	(")	–	44ft.	4½	ins
20	–	(")	–	41ft.	1½	ins
21	–	(")	–	41ft.	4	ins
22	–	(")	–	40ft.	6	ins
24	–	(")	–	36ft.	6	ins
28	–	(Standing Style)	–	31ft.	4½	ins
28	–	(7ft. 6 ins. run)	–	34ft.	1½	ins
36	–	(")	–	28ft.	5½	ins
42	–	(")	–	26ft.	1½	ins
56	–	(")	–	20ft.	8	ins

THROWING THE WEIGHT

28	–	(half turn of body)	–	66ft.	0½	ins
36	–	(")	–	34ft.	1	ins

THROWING THE HAMMER

18	–	(Standing Style)	–	122ft.	12½	ins
25	–	(")	–	100ft.	9	ins

Maps

The very inaccurate outline drawn from Ptolemy's tables of AD 150, was the basis of every map of Britain, until 1546. The first published map of Scotland alone may be one printed in Italy, in 1568, following James V's voyage to the Hebrides 30 years earlier.

After the first Jacobite Rising, much surveying work was done to strengthen the military forts and improve communications through road-building, started in 1725, by General Wade. The picketing and patrolling of Scotland by government troops produced better details and Elphinstone's map of 1745 marks the end of the previous virtual monopoly of the Dutch cartographers. At least three surveys preceded the construction of the Caledonian Canal, an immense and costly project started in 1804, to link the east and west coasts and avoid the danger to sailing ships going round the north of Scotland. It was opened in 1822, and is still operational now, but never carried the traffic envisaged by its engineer, Thomas Telford, as steam power reduced the need for it and ship owners objected to paying passage dues.

Communications & Industry

Lord Abinger, the builder of Torlundy Castle, now the Inverlochy Castle Hotel, cut the first sod of the West Highland Railway, on 23rd October 1889. Thousands of tons of materials were brought by sea for the project, originally estimated to cost £393,638 4s 2d. Before the line opened, the nearest railhead was 6½ hrs away by coach. When the necessary Parliamentary Bill was passed, Fort William heard the news from the bellman and celebrated with a torchlight procession. The railway company ran a horse-drawn bus service to Ballachulish Ferry and Fort William had a regular paddle steamer connection with Oban.

The spade used to cut the first sod of the West Highland Railway on October 23rd 1889.

The ceremonial opening of The West Highland Railway in 1894. Notice the huge draped plate cameras focusing on the dignitaries adjacent to the steam locomotive, left.

In 1896 Fort William became the first town in the United Kingdom to have electric street lighting entirely generated by water power. The same year, aluminium was first produced in this country in commercial quantities using the electrolytic method. The British Aluminium Company pioneered the industrial use of hydro-electric power at Foyers and, in 1904, built a smelter at Kinlochleven, damming the Blackwater River. By 1924 the Fort William reduction works were under construction. Water was brought from Loch Treig and Loch Laggan through a 15 ft diameter tunnel cut through the Ben Nevis range. It is 15 miles long and is the largest tunnel of its kind in Europe. Bauxite is the chief ore in the manufacture of aluminium. It is named after les Baux in southern France. Initially, the Company brought it in from Northern Ireland, but later it came from Ghana through Burntisland on the Firth of Forth and it now comes mainly from the West Indies.

A 1200lb slab of aluminium manufactured in Lochaber.

The piped water also served the pulp and paper mill at Annat Point, opened by Wiggins Teape in 1966. This Government-subsidised enterprise once processed daily 1,000 tons of Scottish timber. Some of the stripped bark was used for fuel and the wood was chipped, chemically treated and washed into white pulp to make high quality paper. The pulp business proved to be uneconomic and now only paper is made at Annat Point.

THE ST. KILDA MAIL BOAT

A sheep's stomach was attached to a hollowed out piece of wood in which were placed letters, wrapped to keep them dry and held in place by a wooden lid. It was floated out into the tide and would come up on the isle of Lewis where the finder would post on the letters through the regular mail service.

Whether you have sent mail by today's more conventional, if less romantic, methods or are keeping postcards to remind you of Lochaber, we hope you have enjoyed your visit.